A TIMELINE OF

WARSHIPS

by **Tim Cooke**

CAPSTONE PRESS
a capstone imprint

Edge Books are published by Capstone Press,
1710 Roe Crest Drive, North Mankato, Minnesota 56003
www.capstonepub.com

Published in 2018 by Capstone Publishing Ltd

Library of Congress Cataloging-in-Publication Data
Cataloging-in-publication information is on file with the Library of Congress.

ISBN: 978-1-5157-9196-6 (library binding)
ISBN: 978-1-5157-9202-4 (eBook PDF)

For Brown Bear Books Ltd:
Managing Editor: Tim Cooke
Designer: John Woolford
Editorial Director: Lindsey Lowe
Design Manager: Keith Davis
Children's Publisher: Anne O'Daly
Picture Manager: Sophie Mortimer
Production Director: Alastair Gourlay

Photo Credits
Front Cover: Department of Defense: tc; Dreamstime: Gannady Poddubny tc;
Getty Images: U.S. Navy b; Library of Congress: cl.
Interior: Alamy: Chronicle 7br, GL Archive 18-19; British Museum London: 6-7b; Central Naval Museum St
Petersburg: 14br; Department of Commerce: 11tr; Department of Defense: 22-23, 24-25, 24bc, 25tr, 26-27, 27tr,
27bc, 28-29, 28bc, 29tr, 29br; Deutsches Museum Munich: 4; Dreamstime: Gannady Poddubny: 6-7t; Duques de
Cardona Collection: 7tr; Getty Images: Science & Society Picture Library 10-11; Glyn1: 5tr; Library of Congress:
13br, 14-15, 15tr; Magdalene College Cambridge: 8-9t; National Archives: 16bc, 25br; Robert Hunt Library: 1, 5bl,
9br, 15bc, 16-17, 17tr, 18bc, 19cr, 20-21, 20br, 21tr, 21bc, 22bc, 23tr, 23bc; Shutterstock: Elenarts 12-13t, RCP Photo
9tr, Michael Rosskothen 5cr; Submarine Force Museum: 11br; United Kingdom Ministry of Defence: 26br.
Artistic effects: Shutterstock

Brown Bear Books has made every attempt to contact the copyright holders.
If you have any information please contact licensing@brownbearbooks.co.uk

Printed in the USA
5607/AG/17

TABLE OF CONTENTS

FIGHTING AT SEA

Early humans began sailing as soon as they learned to strap logs together with reeds to make a raft. Rafts floated because of the natural **buoyancy** of the logs. The earliest boats were used in rivers and along coastlines. It was not until the Phoenicians, who lived in what are now Lebanon and Syria around 3,500 years ago, that ancient people developed ships that could travel long distances.

Archeologists think that all warships developed from just three basic types. These were flat rafts, dugout canoes made from hollow logs, and boats made from bark or animal skins. Submarines, or underwater craft, are much newer inventions. Ships have been used for fighting since ancient times. Submarines have been used for warfare for over 250 years.

THE FIRST SEA POWERS

In ancient Greece and Rome, water transportation was the quickest way to get around. Both the Greeks and Romans built large empires across the world, linked by shipping routes. Heavy sailing ships moved cargo, such as grain, food, or wood. Early warships were lighter and faster, and were usually powered by groups of rowers.

BENEATH THE WAVES

The first practical submarine was built by the Dutch inventor Cornelis Drebbel in 1620. It was a sealed rowboat powered by oars. The vessel had a test voyage on the Thames River in London, England. It would be another 150 years before a submarine was used in warfare.

SEA RAIDERS

From the 700s to the 1000s, Viking warriors from Scandinavia sailed along the coasts of northern Europe in longboats. They landed on beaches and raided coastal communities and churches.

GUNBOAT BULLIES

From the 1700s onward, Western powers used military technology to try to influence other parts of the world. In 1853, for example, U.S. Commodore Matthew Perry sailed a gunboat to Japan. He forced the Japanese to open their markets to U.S. traders.

buoyancy—the ability to float in water
archeologist—a scientist who studies the past

FIRST WARSHIPS

Warships are designed to fight at sea. More than 2,000 years ago, the ancient Greeks designed a warship called a galley. Galleys remained in use in naval battles until the 1500s.

Galleys were long, narrow wooden ships. They carried sails but were mainly powered by large numbers of rowers with oars. A bireme galley had two rows of rowers on each side. A trireme galley had three. A drummer on deck beat time so the men all rowed together. In battle, galleys rammed enemy ships at high speed. A sharp point at the front holed the enemy vessel, which flooded and sank. Galleys also carried soldiers who could board enemy vessels and fight with swords.

THE SAILS were taken down in battles to make the ship easier to maneuver.

TIMELINE

1600 BEFORE THE COMMON ERA (BCE)
THE FIRST NAVY
The Minoan people of the Mediterranean island of Crete build what is probably the first navy anywhere in the world.

1175 BCE
BATTLE AT SEA
The Battle of the Delta takes place between the Egyptians and invaders known as the Sea Peoples. It is one of the first recorded naval battles.

600s BCE
LENDING SHIPS
The Phoenicians of the eastern Mediterranean supply the Persians with sea vessels in order to fight the ancient Greeks.

SPECIFICATIONS

BIREME

Weight: 28.6 tons (26 metric tons)
Length: 83 feet 4 inches
(25.4 meters)
Crew: 50 oarsmen plus 3 officers
Main armament: Bronze **ram**
at front
Top speed: 5 knots (5.8 miles/
9.3 kilometers per hour)
Propulsion: Square sails,
50 oarsmen

IN ACTION

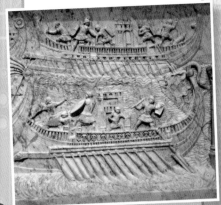

A PAINTED EYE at the front of the galley was intended to protect the ship from the "evil eye." It may also have been meant to frighten the enemy.

FIGHTING GALLEYS

Galleys were fitted with an underwater metal point at the front of the ship. The oarsmen rowed at top speed into the side of the enemy ship. The galley's battering ram smashed into its wooden hull, making a hole and causing it to sink.

THE BRONZE RAM was the only part of the ship that was not made from wood.

480 BCE

GREEK VICTORY

Persian and Greek naval ships clash in a narrow sea channel in the Battle of Salamis. The Greeks sink some 200 Persian galleys.

maneuver—to steer something on a complex course
ram—a long point used to crash into something

GALLEONS

In the 1400s and 1500s, new warships appeared that relied on wind power rather than oars. These galleons had sets of sails to catch the wind. Raised sections called "castles" were built at the back and front to hold the crew.

Galleons were fast and easy to steer. They carried cannons on both sides and at the back that fired cannon balls at enemy ships. The cannons were arranged in rows and fired through holes called gun ports. Each gun had a crew of four. The *Mary Rose* was built for King Henry VIII of England in 1511. In 1545 the ship was leading an English attack on French galleys when it sank. The wreck was raised from the seabed in 1982. It was **preserved** and is now in a museum.

HIGH "CASTLES" at the front and back of the ship. The low middle had an open deck.

TIMELINE

793
SEA RAIDERS
Viking warriors in longboats raid Lindisfarne, a monastery in northern England. It is the first known raid on the coasts of Europe.

1545
FLAGSHIP SINKS
The *Mary Rose*, flagship of the English **fleet**, sinks while fighting French ships. It is thought that water poured in through the ship's open gun ports.

1571
GALLEYS CLASH
The Battle of Lepanto in the Mediterranean Sea is the last battle between galleys. A fleet of combined European powers defeat the fleet of the Ottoman Turks.

SPECIFICATIONS

MARY ROSE
Weight: 700–800 tons
  (635–725 metric tons)
Length: 147 feet 7 inches
  (45 meters)
Propulsion: Sail
Crew: 200 sailors, 185 soldiers,
  30 gunners
Main armament: 78 to 91 guns
Speed: Not known

INSIDE OUT

CROW'S NESTS
at the tops of the masts were used as lookout posts at sea.

SAIL POWER

Sails are mounted on long horizontal poles called booms. The booms can be turned almost lengthwise along the ship to catch more wind in the sails. The more the sails are unfurled, the faster a ship travels. Triangular lateen sails at the front enable the ship to move forward even if the wind is blowing directly toward it.

GUN PORTS
with shutters allowed the ship to carry heavy cannon close to the waterline.

1588

SPANISH ARMADA

The English, led by Sir Francis Drake, defeat a Spanish invasion fleet known as the Armada. The victory leaves England's Royal Navy as the world's leading naval power.

preserve—to stop something from decaying
fleet—a large group of naval ships

FIRST SUBMARINES

Submarines are any ships that move underwater. As early as the 1620s, the Dutch inventor Cornelis Drebbel rowed a submarine in the Thames River. In warfare, submarines make it possible to surprise the enemy.

The first military submarine was used in 1776, during the Revolutionary War (1775–1783). Its American inventor, David Bushnell, called it the *Turtle* because of its shape. The operator let water into a tank to make the vessel sink and pumped the water back out to rise to the surface. Hand-cranked propellers moved the vessel underwater. Bushnell designed the *Turtle* to plant **mines** on British ships. The mines were meant to blow up and sink the ships. However, the *Turtle* was never successful in sinking a vessel.

THE MINE can be detatched for attaching to enemy ships.

TIMELINE

1680
BOMBSHELL
The French invent a new type of warship that carries mortars. These guns fire shells in a high arc. When the shells fall onto a target, they explode.

1761
TIMEKEEPER
British clockmaker John Harrison invents an accurate marine chronometer. The device allows sailors to figure out their longitude, or east/west position, at sea.

SPECIFICATIONS

THE *TURTLE*

Weight: unknown, but included 200 pounds (90.7 kilograms) of lead

Length: 10 feet (3 meters)

Propulsion: Hand-cranked propellers

Crew: One

Main armament: detachable mine

Speed: 2.6 knots (3 miles/4.8 kilometers per hour)

POWER PEOPLE

DAVID BUSHNELL

American inventor David Bushnell invented the *Turtle* while he was a student at Yale University. His idea was to pump water in and out of the vessel to enable it to sink or rise in the water. As well as being an inventor, Bushnell served in the Continental Army during the Revolutionary War.

SMALL PORTHOLES
allowed the *Turtle's* operator to see underwater.

THE FRONT PROPELLER
pulled the *Turtle* forward. The other propeller moved the submarine up or down in the water.

1757 ▷▷▷

A NEW DEVICE
John Bird makes the first sextant. The tool allows sailors to plot their position using the stars.

1775 ▷▷▷

SUBMARINE DEBUT
The *Turtle* is used to try to sink the British warship HMS *Eagle* on September 6, during the Revolutionary War.

mine—a small bomb that sometimes floats in water

SHIPS OF THE LINE

By the middle of the 1700s, the galleon had developed into what was called a ship of the line. With these powerful sailing ships, the British Royal Navy dominated naval warfare for more than 100 years.

One of the Royal Navy's greatest warships was the HMS *Victory*. Like other ships of the line, the *Victory* was designed to operate in a long line of warships. As they sailed toward the enemy, the ships turned and opened fire with all their cannons on the side facing the enemy. This volley of fire was called a broadside. The fleets with the heaviest broadsides usually won a naval battle, so ships were built to carry as many cannons as possible. The *Victory* was launched in 1765. Its most famous success was at the Battle of Trafalgar in 1805.

> **THE SIDES** were painted black and pale orange. The Royal Navy later adopted the color scheme on all its warships.

TIMELINE

1790

SWEDISH VICTORY

A Swedish fleet defeats a Russian fleet in the Battle of Svenskund in the Gulf of Finland. It is the last naval battle involving rowed galleys.

1805

TRAFALGAR

Admiral Lord Horatio Nelson, onboard the HMS *Victory*, defeats French and Spanish navies in the Battle of Trafalgar.

SPECIFICATIONS

HMS VICTORY
Weight: 3,500 tons
(3,175 metric tons)
Length: 227 feet 6 inches
(69.3 meters)
Propulsion: Sail
Crew: 850
Main armament: 104 guns
Speed: 11 knots (12 miles/
20 kilometers per hour)

THE FLAGSHIP carried the admiral in charge of the whole fleet, as well as its own captain.

52 GUNS were arranged in three rows along each side. Each gun could fire a solid, cast-iron cannonball up to 2 miles (3 km).

THE BASE OF THE HULL was covered in copper to stop weeds and **barnacles** from damaging it.

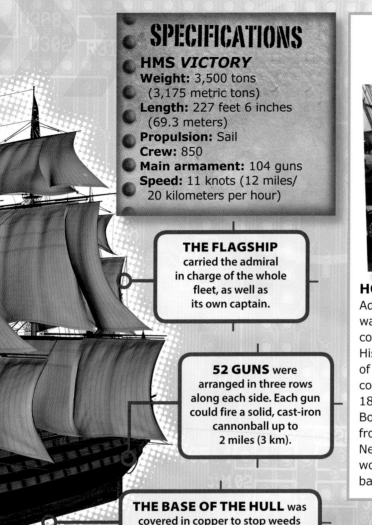

POWER PEOPLE

HORATIO NELSON
Admiral Lord Nelson was the most famous commander of HMS *Victory*. His success at the Battle of Trafalgar off the Spanish coast on October 21, 1805, stopped Napoleon Bonaparte's French army from invading Britain. Nelson was **fatally** wounded during the battle and died a hero.

1807 ⟩⟩⟩
GUNBOAT WAR
In a seven-year conflict, Danish and Norwegian navies try to defeat British ships using many small gunboats. The tactic is usually unsuccessful.

1815 ⟩⟩⟩
STEAM WARSHIP
The United States is the first country to build a warship with a steam engine. Designed by Robert Fulton, it is known as *Demologos* or as *Fulton's No 1*.

barnacle—a small shellfish that sticks to underwater surfaces
fatally—in a way that causes someone to die

IRONCLADS

In the 1800s new cannon shells were developed that could easily pierce wooden hulls. In 1860 the French Navy launched a warship protected by sheets of iron bolted onto its sides. These ships were named "ironclads."

When the U.S. Civil War (1861–1865) began in 1861, both sides built ironclads. The designs were very different from each other. Some of the ships sat very low in the water. Others, like the USS *New Ironsides*, looked more like regular sailing ships. In March 1862, Union and Confederate ironclads met in the Battle of Hampton Roads. It was the first time two iron ships had fought each other. From the 1890s, warships were made of steel rather than wood and iron.

THREE MASTS were used for long-distance sailing. They were removed before any fighting.

SIDES were covered in 4.5-inch (114-mm) thick iron for protection.

TIMELINE

1824
STEAM IN WAR
The first steamship is used in action when the *Diana*, a ship of the English East India Company, fights pirates in Southeast Asia.

1853
END OF WOOD
At the Battle of Sinope, a Russian fleet destroys a wooden Turkish fleet with explosive shells. Navies around the world begin to protect their ships with iron armor.

EYEWITNESS

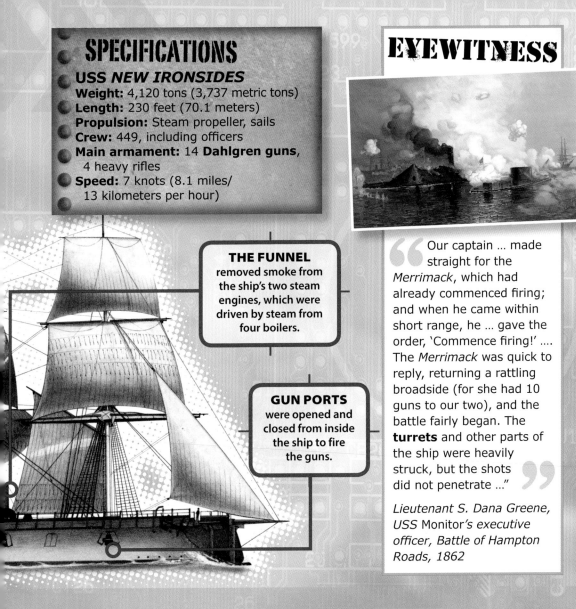

THE FUNNEL removed smoke from the ship's two steam engines, which were driven by steam from four boilers.

GUN PORTS were opened and closed from inside the ship to fire the guns.

> Our captain ... made straight for the *Merrimack*, which had already commenced firing; and when he came within short range, he ... gave the order, 'Commence firing!' .... The *Merrimack* was quick to reply, returning a rattling broadside (for she had 10 guns to our two), and the battle fairly began. The **turrets** and other parts of the ship were heavily struck, but the shots did not penetrate ..."

Lieutenant S. Dana Greene, USS *Monitor's executive officer, Battle of Hampton Roads, 1862*

1859 ≫≫≫

FIRST IRONCLAD
The French Navy launches the first ironclad warship, named *La Gloire*.

1862 ≫≫≫

HAMPTON ROADS
Ironclads fight in the Battle of Hampton Roads in the U.S. Civil War. The battle ends without a clear result.

Dahlgren gun—a large cannon carried on a warship
turret—a raised defensive block

DREADNOUGHTS

In 1906 Britain's Royal Navy introduced the world's fastest and most heavily armed warship the *Dreadnought*. Its name meant "fear nothing." The ship created a new class of ships known as dreadnoughts or battleships.

The HMS *Dreadnought* carried up to 10 huge naval guns that could fire shells up to 14.2 miles (22.8 km), making it the most powerful of all warships. Dreadnoughts were also the first large warships to be powered by steam **turbines**, and they were the fastest warships of their day. By the time World War I (1914–1918) broke out in 1914, all of Europe's leading countries had dreadnoughts. Britain had 29, and Germany had 17.

THREE-LEGGED masts held equipment to transmit details of targets and range to the gun turrets.

SUPERSTRUCTURE was also protected by thick armor.

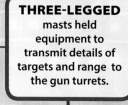

TIMELINE

1863

ILL-FATED SUB
On February 17, the Confederate submarine CSS *Hunley* becomes the first submarine to sink a ship. The *Hunley* then sinks, killing its entire crew.

1880s

MACHINE GUN
Several navies mount Gatling guns on the decks of warships. They use the machine guns against torpedo boat attacks.

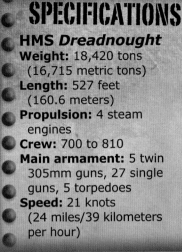

SPECIFICATIONS

HMS *Dreadnought*
Weight: 18,420 tons
(16,715 metric tons)
Length: 527 feet
(160.6 meters)
Propulsion: 4 steam
engines
Crew: 700 to 810
Main armament: 5 twin
305mm guns, 27 single
guns, 5 torpedoes
Speed: 21 knots
(24 miles/39 kilometers
per hour)

INSIDE OUT

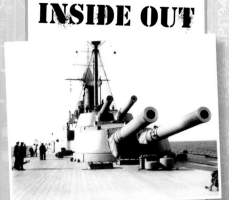

NAVAL GUNS

Dreadnoughts carried huge guns and shells. Each gun required a crew of up to 50 gunners to load, aim, and fire it. The gun crew all had different tasks, including loading shells and explosive powder into the back of the guns and adjusting the direction of the guns between firing.

HULL ARMOR was 11 inches (28 centimeters) thick at its widest point, around the **waterline**.

1900 ⟫⟫

HOLLAND CLASS
Britain's Royal Navy launches its first successful submarine, the *Holland*. It builds five of the vessels, but they are too unreliable to go into service.

1906

A REVOLUTION
The Royal Navy launches the first battleship, the HMS *Dreadnought*. The ship greatly changes naval warfare. A race begins to build similar ships in Europe and around the world.

turbine—a machine that generates power from a stream of air or steam
waterline—the level the sea reaches on a ship

U-BOATS

During World War I, the German navy used submarines known as U-boats, short for *Unterseeboot*. The name was German for "underwater boat." These U-boats attacked ships sailing to Europe from the United States.

> **THE CREW** lived and slept in a tiny compartment toward the rear of the submarine.

The U-boats spent up to five days at a time patrolling the waters of the Atlantic Ocean and the English Channel. They only had enough air to stay **submerged** for two hours. When they were close enough to surprise an enemy ship, the U-boats usually surfaced to attack. The German use of submarines outraged many people, who thought submarine attacks went against the unwritten "rules" of conflict. German U-boat attacks on U.S. ships were one reason why the United States entered World War I in April 1917.

TIMELINE

1910
AIR POWER AT SEA
U.S. pilot Eugene Ely becomes the first man to take off successfully in an airplane from the deck of an anchored battleship, the USS *Birmingham*.

1915
LUSITANIA SINKS
The U-boat *U-20* sinks the passenger liner RMS *Lusitania*. Almost 1,200 people die. They include 128 Americans.

SPECIFICATIONS

Type UB1 Coastal U-Boat
Weight: 142 tons (128 metric tons)
Length: 92 feet 2 inches
(28.10 meters)
Propulsion: diesel engine,
propeller shaft
Crew: 14
Main armament: 2 torpedo tubes,
machine gun
Speed: 5.5 knots (6.3 miles/
10.2 kilometers per hour)

POWER PEOPLE

REINHARD SCHEER
Known as the "man with the mask" for his fierce appearance, Reinhard Scheer was an admiral in the Imperial German Navy. Scheer was one of the first men to understand the importance of submarines in modern warfare. He persuaded the German goverment to let U-boats attack any targets without warning during World War I.

THE CONNING TOWER
acted as a lookout position when the submarine was on the surface.

THE TORPEDO
tubes were at the front of the vessel.

1916 》》

NAVAL BATTLE
The only major naval clash of World War I takes place in the North Sea from May 31 to June 1. The battle ends in a British victory.

1917

CONVOY SYSTEM
Merchant ships sailing to Britain begin to cross the Atlantic Ocean in **convoys** guarded by warships and aircraft. The system helps prevent U-boat attacks.

submerge—to go below the surface of the water
convoy—a group of ships traveling together

AIRCRAFT CARRIERS

After World War I, aircraft carriers were developed as floating airbases. They had flat decks to allow airplanes to take off and land. In World War II (1939–1945) aircraft carriers were vital in the Pacific War against Japan.

In December 1941, the Japanese tried to destroy the U.S. aircraft carriers by attacking their base at Pearl Harbor. By chance, the carriers were out at sea and escaped the attack. The aircraft carriers became the basis of the military campaign against Japan. U.S. factories made more than 100 carriers during the war. U.S. commanders used them to launch **airstrikes** on islands held by the Japanese and on Japan itself.

THE FLIGHT DECK has two runways. One deck has a **catapult** to launch planes into the air. The other deck is at an angle to help planes land.

AN ELEVATOR allows aircraft to be stored in a hangar beneath the deck and brought up when needed.

TIMELINE

1918

TOP SUBMARINE
By the time World War I ends in November, the most successful German U-boat, *U-35*, has sunk 324 Allied merchant ships.

1941

JAPANESE RAID
On December 7, Japanese airplanes bomb the U.S. naval base at Pearl Harbor in Hawaii. The next day, the United States enters World War II.

SPECIFICATIONS

USS *ESSEX*
Weight: 36,380 tons
(33,003 metric tons)
Length: 872 feet (266 meters)
Propulsion: 8 boilers,
4 steam turbines, 4 shafts
Crew: 2,600 officers +
enlisted men
Main armament: 4 twin 127mm
guns, 4 single 127mm guns,
8 quadruple 40mm guns,
46 single 20mm guns
Speed: 33 knots (38 miles/
61 kilometers per hour)

THE CONTROL center is in a turret positioned on the edge of the deck to allow for the longest runway possible.

IN ACTION

BATTLE OF MIDWAY

From June 4 to June 7 in 1942, the U.S. and Japanese fleets clashed near Midway Island in the Pacific Ocean. The Battle of Midway was fought entirely by aircraft from carriers. Although one U.S. carrier was sunk, U.S. aircraft sank four Japanese aircraft carriers. The Imperial Japanese Navy never recovered from the defeat.

1942

OUT OF SIGHT
The Battle of the Coral Sea (May 4–8) is the first aircraft carrier battle. The U.S. and Japanese fleets never meet as their aircraft fight overhead.

1942

CARRIER WARFARE
In the Battle of Midway, U.S. bombers sink Japan's aircraft carrier *Akagi*. Carriers have now replaced battleships as the basis of naval power.

catapult—a device used to launch aircraft from the decks of ships
airstrike—an attack carried out by airplanes with bombs and missiles

NEW BATTLESHIPS

As aircraft carriers became more important in the Pacific in World War II, the U.S. Navy built new battleships to protect them. These fast battleships defended the carriers. They also bombarded Japanese defenses on Pacific islands.

U.S. shipyards built four new Iowa-class battleships, named for the first ship in the class, the USS *Iowa*. As U.S. forces advanced toward Japan, they captured Japanese-held islands to serve as airbases. Iowa-class ships such as the USS *New Jersey* fired at Japanese positions from **offshore**. Then U.S. soldiers and Marines made **amphibious** landings on the beaches. The USS *Iowa* also served in the Atlantic Ocean, when it took President Franklin D. Roosevelt to a meeting with British Prime Minister Winston Churchill and Soviet leader Joseph Stalin in 1943.

TIMELINE

1943

THE TIDE TURNS
In May increased Allied airpower and other measures result in more U-boats being sunk and fewer losses of Allied ships.

1944

D-DAY INVASION
Around 1,200 warships, 4,120 landing ships, and 1,500 other vessels take part in the D-Day landings in Normandy, France, on June 6.

SPECIFICATIONS

USS *New Jersey*
Weight: 58,000 tons
(52,600 metric tons)
Length: 887 feet 7 inches
(270.5 meters)
Crew: 1,921 officers and men
Main armament: 9 16-inch guns,
20 5-inch guns,
129 antiaircraft guns
Speed: 33 knots (37.9 miles/
61 kilometers per hour)

INSIDE OUT

BIG GUNS

The nine 16-inch (40.4-cm) guns of the Iowa-class battleships were housed in three gun turrets. Each turret had a crew of 79 men. The guns could be aimed and fired separately. The shells weighed up to 2,700 pounds (1,200 kg). They had a range of up to 24 miles (39 km).

ANTIAIRCRAFT GUNS
protected the ship from *kamikaze* pilots — Japanese pilots who deliberately tried to crash their planes into U.S. ships.

THE GUNS were 50 times as long as they were wide. They measured 66.6 feet (20 m) long.

1945 ≫≫≫

END OF THE WAR
On September 2, the Japanese surrender in an official ceremony onboard the Iowa-class USS *Missouri*, formally ending World War II.

1950

SOVIET BUILDUP
The Soviet Union starts to build the world's largest submarine fleet.

offshore—in the sea close to the coast
amphibious—moving between the sea and the land

NUCLEAR SUBMARINES

In the 1950s the United States built the first nuclear-powered submarines. They could stay submerged for months at a time. The first, the USS *Nautilus*, was launched in 1954.

During the Cold War (1947–1991), both the United States and the Soviet Union competed for political influence around the world. They both built **nuclear** submarines. The submarines carried missiles armed with nuclear bombs. If a nuclear war broke out between the two countries, nuclear submarines at sea would strike back at whoever had launched the original attack. The biggest U.S. nuclear submarines ever built were the Ohio Class, but the most numerous belonged to the Los Angeles class, like the USS *Louisville*.

THE PROPELLER works quietly and produces few bubbles. That makes it difficult for other vessels to hear the submarine approaching.

NUCLEAR REACTOR held in radiation-proof casing. The reactor only needs to be refueled every 12 to 15 years.

TIMELINE

1954

NUCLEAR POWER
The United States launches the world's first nuclear-powered vessel, the USS *Nautilus* submarine.

1962

CONFRONTATION
U.S. warships stop and search Soviet ships heading toward Cuba to check that they are not carrying missiles.

SPECIFICATIONS

USS *Louisville*
Weight: 6,818 tons
(6,185 metric tons)
Length: 362 feet
(110 meters)
Propulsion: 1 nuclear
reactor, 2 turbines,
1 motor shaft
Crew: 129
Main armament:
37 Mark 48 torpedoes,
Tomahawk missile
Speed: 20 knots (23 miles/
37 kilometers per hour)

INSIDE OUT

NUCLEAR POWER

Nuclear reactors are ideal
for submarines because
they do not need oxygen
to operate. They work by
splitting heavy **atoms**,
such as uranium, into
lighter atoms. This process
releases a huge amount of
energy as heat. The process
is called nuclear fission.

CONNING TOWER
holds a **periscope** and a
snorkel that allows the
submarine to run its
emergency diesel engine.

CREW LIVING
COMPARTMENTS
are all at the front of
the submarine.

1965 〉〉〉

WAR IN VIETNAM
At the start of the Vietnam
War (1955–1975), U.S.
aircraft carriers act
as air bases off the
Vietnamese coast.

1965

BROWN WATER
Fast Patrol Craft (FPC)
carry out missions on the
many rivers of Vietnam.
The ships are known as
the Brown Water Navy.

nuclear—using energy released from atoms
periscope—a tube with mirrors for viewing things above one's height
atom—the smallest particle of a chemical

25

SUPERCARRIERS

Modern supercarriers are the biggest warships in the world. They can transport up to 90 airplanes and helicopters to combat zones. Supercarriers are like mini-cities. More than 5,000 crew live on board at any one time.

Supercarriers have a short takeoff deck at the front. They use a catapult to throw fighter planes into the air. The landing deck is a diagonal strip running from the back of the ship. These two runways allow planes to take off and land at the same time. The biggest supercarriers belong to the Nimitz class, which entered service in 1975. Supercarriers carry few weapons of their own. They are protected at sea by a **battle group** of warships such as destroyers.

TAKE-OFF deck is at the front of the ship. The area can also be used to store and maintain aircraft.

TIMELINE

1975
BIGGEST SHIPS
The Nimitz class of aircraft carrier enters service. Ten are built before the last is commissioned in 2009.

1982
WAR AT SEA
The Falklands War (1982) is the largest naval campaign since World War II. Great Britain goes to war with Argentina in the South Atlantic Ocean.

SPECIFICATIONS

NIMITZ CLASS

Weight: 117,150 tons
(106,280 metric tons)
Length: 1,092 feet (332.8 meters)
Propulsion: 2 nuclear reactors,
4 shafts, 4 steam turbines
Crew: 5,000+
Main armament: Up to 24 Sea
Sparrow antiaircraft, antimissile
missiles, 3 or 4 defense missiles
Speed: 30+ knots (35 miles/
56 kilometers per hour)

EYEWITNESS

" In some ways I hate
the night catapult
shot more than I hate the
night landing. You sit there,
they dim the lights down
but your eyes take time to
adjust. They shoot you off
the front end and on a dark
night you've got no visual
reference, no idea where
the horizon is. It's like
getting shot into a black
hole. You only have your
instruments to trust. "

*"Disney," nickname
of a pilot onboard the
supercarrier USS* George
H.W. Bush

ARRESTER WIRES
across the landing deck
catch a hook dropped by an
airplane to slow it down.

THE LANDING DECK slopes at
a 9-degree angle to make it easier
for pilots to land.

1985

STEALTH SHIP

The U.S. Navy reveals
its first **stealth** ship,
Sea Shadow. The ship is
designed to be more
difficult to detect by
enemy technology.

2000

DISASTER

The Russian attack
submarine *Kursk* sinks
while sailing in the
Barents Sea. All 118
officers and crew die
in the disaster.

battle group—a number of warships that travel and fight together
stealth—ways to make vessels difficult to detect

NEW GENERATION

Warships, aircraft carriers, and submarines continue to play a key role in military defense. Designers of the new generation of warships and submarines use new technologies and materials to create ships that are virtually invisible.

The latest stealth technology makes ships as hard to detect as possible. Vessels such as the U.S. Independence class of combat ships can enter enemy territory unseen. They patrol coasts or deliver special forces into war zones. New technology has also taken over many naval jobs. On submarines, this means fewer crew are needed on board, with fewer supplies. That enables submarines to undertake longer missions.

REAR DECK is a launchpad for two Seahawk helicopters and an unmanned Sea Scout drone.

INTO THE FUTURE

NEW SUPERCARRIER
The U.S. Navy is building the new Gerald R. Ford class of supercarriers. The carriers will be able to launch more aircraft than any other type of aircraft carrier, using fewer personnel.

SPECIFICATIONS

**USS *Independence*
LCS-2**
Weight: 878.5 tons
(797 metric tons)
Length: 418 feet
(127.4 meters)
Propulsion: 2 diesel
engines, 2 gas turbines
Crew: 43 + up to 35 crew
Main armament: Missiles,
5 guns
Speed: 44 knots
(51 miles/81 kilometers
per hour)

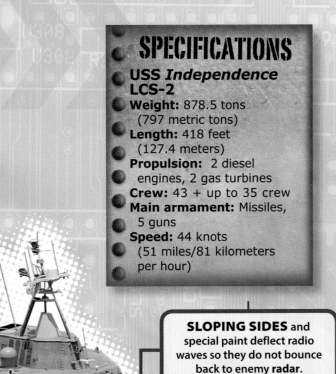

SLOPING SIDES and special paint deflect radio waves so they do not bounce back to enemy **radar**.

INSIDE OUT

STEALTH SHIPS
Stealth ships have special absorbent materials on their hulls that absorb radio waves. Some also have sloping sides that deflect radio waves. Both these defenses prevent radio signals betraying the ships' position to enemy radar.

HULL DIVIDED into three. This trimaran design cuts water resistance, so the vessel uses less fuel.

ATTACK VESSEL
The M80 Stiletto is a new U.S. stealth ship. Its hull is built from carbon fiber, which does not show up on radar. The ship is partly designed to land special forces on enemy coasts without being detected.

drone—an unpiloted flying vehicle
radar—a device that locates objects by bouncing radio waves off them

29

GLOSSARY

airstrike (AIR-strike)—an attack carried out by airplanes with bombs and missiles

amphibious (am-FIB-ee-us)—moving between the sea and the land

archeologist (ar-key-AHL-uh-jist)—a scientist who studies the past

atom (AH-tum)—the smallest particle of a chemical

barnacle (BAR-nuh-cul)—a small shellfish that sticks to underwater surfaces

battle group (BAH-tul GROOP)—a number of warships that travel and fight together

buoyancy (BOY-un-cee)—the ability to float in water

catapult (CAT-ah-PULT)—a device used to launch aircraft from the decks of ships

convoy (CON-voy)—a group of ships traveling together

Dahlgren gun (DALL-grun GUN)—a large cannon carried on warships

drone (DROHN)—an unpiloted flying vehicle

fatally (FAY-tul-lee)—in a way that causes someone to die

fleet (FLEET)—a large group of naval ships

maneuver (man-OO-ver)—to steer something on a complex course

mine (MYN)—a small bomb that sometimes floats in water

nuclear (NOO-clee-ur)—using energy released from atoms

offshore (OFF-shore)—in the sea close to the coast

periscope (PARE-uh-scope)—a tube with mirrors for viewing things above one's own height

preserve (pru-SERVE)—to stop something from decaying

radar (RAY-dar)—a device that locates objects by bouncing radio waves off them

ram (RAM)—a long point used to crash into something

stealth (STELTH)—ways to make vessels difficult to detect

submerge (sub-MERJ)—to go below the surface of the water

turbine (TER-byn)—a machine that generates power from a stream of air or steam

turret (TUR-ruht)—a raised defensive block

waterline (WAHT-uhr-line)—the level the sea reaches on a ship

READ MORE

Colson, Rob. *Warships*. Ultimate Machines.
New York: PowerKids Press, 2013

Marisco, Katie. *Warships*. True Bookengineering Wonders.
New York: Children's Press, 2016

Mavrikis, Peter. *What's Inside Classic Warships?*
What's Inside? New York: PowerKids Press, 2016

Stark, William N. *Mighty Military Ships*. Military Machines on Duty.
North Mankato, Minn.: Capstone Press, 2016

INTERNET SITES

Use FactHound to find Internet sites
related to this book.

Visit www.facthound.com

Just type in 9781515791966 and go.

Super-cool stuff!

Check out projects, games and lots more at
www.capstonekids.com

INDEX